NO SWEAT!
Elevator Speech

How to Craft
Your Elevator Speech,
Floor by Floor, with -
NO SWEAT!

By
Fred E. Miller

http://www.nosweatpublicspeaking.com

NO SWEAT! Elevator Speech!
How to Craft Your Elevator Speech, Floor by Floor, with - NO SWEAT!

Published by Fred Co., St. Louis, MO.

Illustrations by Charles Manion. Copyright © 2014 by Charles Manion. All rights reserved.

Book design kenjoymedia.com

To order additional copies of this title, contact https://www.amazon.com/author/fredemiller

The author may be contacted through his website http://www.nosweatpublicspeaking.com.

Printed in the United States of America.
First Printing, 2012.
Second Printing, 2014.

ISBN-13: 978-0-9843967-7-1
1. Public Speaking 2. Presentations 3. Business

Table of Contents

Speaking Opportunities
are Business, Career, and Leadership
Opportunities!

—*Fred E. Miller*

Dedication

This book is dedicated to everyone who ever struggled with their Elevator Speech.

It's for all who stutter, stammer, and generally embarrass themselves when answering the question:
"What do you do?"

Don't give up!
This book holds the answer

Read it - Study it - Practice it
and *your* Elevator Speech will be
NO SWEAT!

Forward

Many of us attend business networking events, social functions, and seminars. We meet new people and reconnect with individuals we know.

It's an opportunity to let everyone know *who* we are and *what* we do. It's also a chance to receive information about *them*. Many offer products and services we, or someone we know, might need now, or later.

Telling people *who* you are and *what* you do is often called an **Elevator Speech**. Many struggle with developing and delivering one. *I did for years.*

I'm in several networking groups. The leader of one of them approached me one day and said, "Fred, You're our Public Speaking, Presentation Expert. At our next gathering, how about giving us a presentation on how to develop a great Elevator Speech?"

"Jeez!" I thought to myself. "I struggle with mine and it *stinks*! You want *me* to show *others* how to create and deliver a great Elevator Speech! *Bummer!"*

I'm a Public Speaking, Presentation Expert. I *should* have a great Elevator Speech and be able to coach others on developing, practicing, and delivering their own.
At that moment I made a decision to get serious, *very* serious, about my Elevator Speech, although I had no idea what my next step would be.

Luckily, the next day, while sitting in my sales class, something occurred that gave me the direction I needed for this task. A classmate of mine, Roy Reichold, gave his Elevator Speech. One thing he said was so profound *everyone* grabbed a pen and wrote it down. That sparked a fire in me to develop my Elevator Speech Template.

Clients and prospects ask me for guidance on this. *Now,* I've got a *proven* formula and template to give them. I want to give it to *you*, too!

The following will help for crafting *your* Elevator Speech. Included is a graphic of the **Elevator Speech Template** I developed.
- Reviewing this graphic will help you "see" the logic of the way it was built.
- Putting those "floors" in "your world" will make customizing easier.

There is also an **Elevator Speech Worksheet**.
- Use it to write your Elevator Speech, floor by floor.

To best benefit from this book:
It will help to have and use the Template and Worksheet as PDFs.

Go Here to Receive the
FREE Elevator Speech Template and
FREE Elevator Speech Worksheet PDFs,
http://www.nosweatpublicspeaking.com/go/
freeelevatorspeechtemplate

Reading the paperback version of this book? Then use a free QR code scanner on your smart phone and scan this code to receive the free templates and worksheets!

No Sweat!
Elevator Speech

Chapter 1 - The Elevator Speech

When I'm addressing an audience, and open a presentation on this subject, I ask, "By a show of hands. "Who, within the last year, has *Changed*, *Trashed,* or *Tweaked* their **Elevator Speech?**
Immediately, many hands go up.

I'll continue, "In the last six *months. . .?*
In the last six *weeks. . .?*
In the last six *days?*
As *I'm speaking* you are . . ."

If you're like most attendees who answer this question, your hand is raised throughout my questioning.

I struggled with my Elevator Speech for years. It was always a "work in progress."

We've all been there: We're attending a networking event, social function, or seminar. The leader announces, *"Before we get started*, let's go around the room and introduce ourselves. Stand up. Tell us *who* you are and *what* you do. Give us your *Elevator Speech."*

For me, this used to be a religious moment. Inside my head I would say, *"Please God*, don't let him call on me first. I know I should have been working on this. I'll be prepared next time. *Please* don't let me embarrass myself by being the first picked!"

At this point, I'm *not* making eye contact with the leader. I'm hoping upon hope someone jumps up and exclaims, *"I'll go first!"*

I'm sure you've never done this, but more than once, I've thought about grabbing my phone, pretending I had an important call, and excusing myself from the group.

Ultimately, someone starts delivering their Elevator Speech, and we feel like a huge weight has been lifted from our shoulders.

Unfortunately, that instant of comfort is usually followed by thoughts of, *"Oh no!* What if the person *just ahead* of me delivers one of those *"Killer"* Elevator Speeches? The kind everyone Oohs! and Ahs! over. That will be *worse than being first!"* That frightful thought is usually followed by a quick glance to the person next to you, and guessing how well *they* will do when it's their turn.

Thus, the speeches begin, and they're usually all over the place in quality and quantity.

A Few Good Ones

Occasionally, we hear some excellent ones that get straight to the point. The person delivering tells us:
- Their name
- Their company's name.
- An item or two that indicate expertise.
- What product(s) and service(s) they offer.
- Something that distinguishes them from others in the same field.

Example:
Hi, everyone!

I'm Bob. I'm an Estate Planning Attorney. This is all I do, and I've done it for over twenty-five years. I've written several articles and pamphlets on the subject. You may have read some of them in local publications.

Living Wills, Trusts, Inheritance Laws: I'm an *expert* in all of them. If you haven't done estate planning, or want a review of the plan you have to see if it's up to date and includes everything it should have in place, *let's have a conversation!"*

Bob seems to "know what he's doing" in this specific area. He's established credibility - a good thing! After hearing his Elevator Speech, we can make a decision if we want to know more, or not. If we do, we'll catch up with him when there's a break, after the event, or later. We're probably comfortable giving his name to others if the subject of Estate Planning comes up in a conversation.

The Really Quick, Short, Boring Ones

These give the minimum amount of information, and *nothing* that grabs our attention or interest.

Example:
"I'm Johnny. I'm an accountant. If you need accounting work, call me."

So what? You've told me nothing that distinguishes you from your competition, or gives me any reason to think you're good at what you do. Why would I want to meet you later and know more? I could never think of referring you, either.

The *Please Sit Down!* Elevator Speeches

This type gives *far* more information than anyone wants to hear. They usually take *more* time to deliver than they are allotted. Their talk is *so far* from what an Elevator Speech should be that we're better off *not* hearing them. Several fall into this obnoxious category:

The Long, Long, Long Ones

At the other end of the Quick, Short, and Boring Elevator Speech is the individual who rambles on and on and on. . .

If they offer ten products, they'll tell you about fifteen! They give several "case studies" about how their product or service changed forever the lives of people or companies who bought it, ignoring three "dings" from the timer of the speeches to STOP! *Finally*, they sit down! They've left little time for others to present within the time allotted for this exercise.

You've experienced these, haven't you? It's a terrible Elevator Speech, and I can't imagine wanting to spend more time with them! If you really were on an elevator with them, you'd be prying the door open to get off or hitting the emergency button!

The Cutesy Ones that *Don't* Say Much

These folks think they can "tease" you into "*wanting* to know more about them and their offering."

Examples:
"I'm Robin, The Financial Plumber for all your money troubles. Work with me, and I'll help you flush those problems out of your life forever!"

or

"I turn men who are Wall Flowers into Chick Magnets!"

You've got to be kidding! What you told me is too vague. I don't want to know more!

The Business Opportunity Ones

These people are usually looking to build a "down line" for their multi-level marketing business. MLM works for many people, but *please*, tell us *very clearly* what you do! The audience isn't filled with mind readers.

Example:
"I'm Susie and I went from being $50,000 in debt to making $10,000 a week, and I'll show YOU how to do it, also!"

Yeah! - I'm sure that's true. (It may be a truthful statement. If so, from the get-go tell us what company helped you accomplish this. What is the product or service you sell?)

One of my problems with that type of elevator speech is that I don't have a clue what they are talking about. If you ask, the response often doesn't directly answer the question. It's usually something like, "Let's set a time and date for coffee and I'll give you the details. Is next Monday morning, at ten o'clock at the downtown Starbucks OK with you?" By this time, they're usually holding their smart phone and hoping to confirm the appointment.

Again, if it's a *business opportunity, tell* us in the Elevator Speech. For some in the audience, that might be a perfect fit.

Going Forward, I'm Going to Cover:

➡ *What* is an Elevator Speech and *Why* have one.
➡ How I developed an **Elevator Speech Template** that works well for me, and will for you, also.
➡ *How* to Deliver an Elevator Speech.
➡ Bonus Tips to take Your Elevator Speech from *Blah* to *Ah!*
➡ The Fear of Public Speaking.
 • It's a big reason people don't like Elevator Speeches!
 • *Why* we have this fear.
 • Nuggets to Lessen it.

Chapter 2 - *What* is an Elevator Speech and *Why* Have One

A Great Elevator Speech
Clearly states:
Who You Are
What You Do.

An Elevator Speech is a personal, mini-infomercial that tells people, very clearly, *who* you are and *what* you do.

The original reason this was called an "Elevator Speech" was that in the time it took an elevator to go to the next floor, you could answer the question, "What do you do?"

With that framework, it had to be short and to the point, usually sixty seconds or less.

I have never delivered an Elevator Speech in an elevator, and don't know anyone who has. That being said, the concept is a good one.

Elevator speeches are *not* meant for selling your products and services. Doing that is definitely not acceptable.
The objective is simple: People hearing it should know *exactly* what you do. *Clarity is not optional.*

When they know what you do, they can make a decision to have conversation with you, or not, about your offering. If they have a clear understanding of your offering(s) and believe you have expertise, they can refer others to you.

Two Distinct Audiences for an Elevator Speech

Elevator Speeches are delivered to two different audiences. They are given to a **Group** or to an **Individual**. Each has specific objectives, different from the other.

One rule they both share is that an **Elevator Speech is not for selling!** An elevator speech is *not* a sales presentation. It *is* a way to let others know who you are and what you offer. Buying and selling, if they occur, must come *later.*

Group

Whenever we attend one of those functions where we have the "opportunity," *yes,* it *is* an opportunity (a *Speaking* Opportunity), to present our Elevator Speech, the **Goal** is:

- *Everyone* hearing it has a *very clear understanding* about our offering. They have enough information to recognize if it's something they, or someone they know, would like more information on.

- They should *not* be trying to decipher what they just heard. They should **GET IT**! *immediately,* when we deliver it. If they are confused by what we said - *it's over!*

The **Goal and Ideal Result of the Group Elevator Speech** is that people approach us during a break or after the event, ask a few questions, and agree to set a time and date for a conversation to gather additional information and determine if they want to buy from us.

An Elevator Speech, presented to a Group, is up to ninety-seconds in length. Because it is built "floor by floor," something we'll discuss later, its length can, if necessary, be modified to meet the time given to this activity when it is presented to a group.

Individual, Face-to-Face

These Elevator Speeches are given in planned and unplanned settings. They happen continually when we meet new people.

The *planned* one often has a directive like this: "Before our scheduled program at 8:00 PM, we have time allotted for networking. Get here by 7:30 and *network!*" Networking can also be done during breaks in the scheduled program and afterwards.

An *unplanned* Elevator Speech can be called upon almost anywhere and anytime. We could be standing in line for a movie, concert, or carnival ride. A conversation is struck up with folks, also waiting, around us. Someone introduces themselves by saying, "I'm Bob. I work over at Home Depot in the Paint Department. What's *your* name, and what do *you* do?"

The Individual, Face-to-Face Elevator Speech has Two Goals:

1. Planned or unplanned, one goal is to *Dis*-qualify the person you're having a conversation with.
   - Everyone is not a prospect for what you offer.
   - You're not a prospect to buy everything presented to you, are you?
   - "Don't spend *major* time on *minor* possibilities." If the person you're speaking with has no interest in what you do, find out *sooner* instead of later. If that's the case, move on to another person and start *dis*qualifying.

2. The second goal and *ideal* result are the individual stops us from talking and says, "Wait. It sounds as if you offer something I might need. I should find

out more about it. Here's my card and give me yours, please. Let's connect in the next few days and set a time to meet and continue this conversation."

The Backstory of *My* Elevator Speech

I've been in Elevator Speech Hell often; tongue-tied and not saying what I wanted to convey on more occasions than I care to admit. I struggled with that important short speech for years. Mine was always a "work in progress." (Can *you* relate to that?)

When someone tells you, *after* your Elevator Speech, they don't know what you do - it's *embarrassing!* I've been there.

I Was *Volunteered!* Here's what happened:

I'm in several networking groups. One of them, Experts for Entrepreneurs, has a dynamic leader, Bill. He approached me one day and said, "Fred, You're our Public Speaking, Presentation Expert. How about giving our group a presentation next month on how to develop a great Elevator Speech?"

"Jeez!" I thought to myself. "Mine *stinks*! It's going to be tough to develop a presentation on something I struggle with. *Bummer!"*

Bill's statement was *not a suggestion*, and was also something I *knew* I absolutely needed to do. I'm a Public Speaking, Presentation Expert. I *should* have a great Elevator Speech and be able to coach others on developing, practicing, and delivering one.

I'm glad he did it because it got me out of my comfort zone. That's a *good thing,* because when we get out of our comfort zone - it becomes *larger!*

At that moment I made a decision to get serious, *very* serious, about my Elevator Speech, although I had no idea what my next step would be.

Luckily, the next day, while sitting in my sales class, something occurred that gave me the punch and direction I needed for this task.

Here's what happened:
We had a new student. As class was starting, and as usually happens when there is a newbie, the instructor said, *"Before we get started,* let's go around the room and introduce ourselves. Stand up. Tell us *who* you are and *what* you do. Give us your *Elevator Speech."*

I blundered through mine, as did most my classmates. However, Roy, who was seated next to me, said something so profound that *everyone* stopped, grabbed a piece of paper, and wrote it down. One sentence in his Elevator Speech made it stand out from all others. **One phrase** in that sentence was strikingly different from the words most of us were using. What Roy said sparked a fire in me to develop my Elevator Speech Template. *Keep reading and I'll tell you what it was!*

Two Words Crafted The Elevator Speech Template

Elevator

As earlier stated, an Elevator Speech is a personal, mini-infomercial that can be delivered to others in an elevator, before it reaches the next floor.

It should clearly and quickly describe what you do.

One thing about the word **Elevator** jumped out at me. It goes up, one floor at a time. It became obvious that an **Elevator** *Speech* should be crafted, *floor-by-floor!*

15

THE ELEVATOR SPEECH
Starts simple.
As interest and time permit,
it is expanded.

Furthermore:
- ➡ Each floor should convey *specific information.*
  - • Start simple. As interest grows (in the Face-to-face), and time permits (in front of individuals and groups), move to the "next floor" and give *more* specific information.
- ➡ For the **Group setting**, we want to take everyone in the room to the top floor, and give them all the information we've crafted for our "Ultimate" Elevator Speech.
  - • Where there are time constraints, some floors can be skipped. (Most elevators don't stop at all floors, do they?)
- ➡ For the **Individual, Face-to-face setting**, we start on the ground floor, and want to take them up, one floor at a time, *only* if interest is shown after we speak.
  - • This is in line with our **One-on-one conviction of not wanting to spend *major* time on *minor* possibilities,** and *Dis*qualifying **people**.

- Some folks are being polite and just want to know our name! That's OK.
- Others will lose interest when they hear what we do. That's OK, also, because this is a great way to *dis*qualify people for your offerings.
- Unless interest is expressed, verbally or nonverbally (body language is extremely important), stop the elevator and move on to someone who might have an interest in your offerings.

Speech

An Elevator Speech is a *Mini-*Presentation. It is a *"Speaking* Opportunity!"* and an important one!

If you've seen me speak, watched my videos, or read my books or posts you know my mantra is, **"*Speaking* Opportunities are *Business, Career,* and *Leadership* Opportunities!"** No one ever challenges that statement. *Why would they!*

Whether delivered to a room full of people, a group gathered around a conference table, or only one person— it *is* a presentation!

Since it *is* a mini-presentation, it should have the same Components, Parts, and Elements of the kind of presentation delivered before an audience in a seminar. We'll look at them in a future chapter.

Like a Swiss Army Knife. . .

The Elevator Speech must be Multipurpose, because. . .

People deliver Elevator Speeches for:
- ➡ Themselves
  - • They may be self-employed or an employee.
  - • They could be unemployed
- ➡ Their workplace, which could be a:
  - • For profit business.
  - • Non profit business.
- ➡ A club, group, or organization.

The Elevator Speech Template has to be *Flexible,* because. . .
➡ Audience size can vary greatly.
➡ Time restraints will differ from being as short as fifteen-seconds to as long as a minute and a half.
➡ It's not just for Elevators! Be prepared to use it on:
  • Escalators.
  • Moving Sidewalks.
  • Stairs.
  • Sidewalks.
  • Bicycle Rides!

The Essence of a Great Elevator Speech

A great Elevator Speech should:
- ➡ Clearly articulate what you do, and if time allows, something that indicates expertise. (We like to work with Experts, don't we!)
- ➡ Be succinct.
- ➡ Have an impact.

Here is the back story, and a great example, of a *non-*Elevator Speech that does that well.

I once had a '98 Ford Explorer. It had a few dings and dents, and over 150,000 miles on it. I loved it. (That minor body damage isn't all bad. People wave you through at four-way stops, and drivers give you greater leeway in parking lots!)

I needed brakes, and was looking for a mechanic I could trust not to push me into repairs I didn't need. I sent requests to friends for recommendations.

Danny's name came up. He worked at a well known, independent garage and moonlighted on the side. I gave him a call. I don't know a lot about cars, and I asked many questions about brakes, and other car related repairs. After answering a few of them, Danny stopped me and gave me one of the best *non-*Elevator Speeches I've ever heard. It's only three short sentences. Here it is:

"Fred, I went to Ranken Technical College. (One of the top career technical training schools in the country.) I'm ASE Certified. (You, like me, have probably seen that logo in professional garages. It stands for Automotive Service Excellence.)

You're in good hands."

"Done!" I said to myself. We had not discussed price. It didn't matter to me. With those few sentences, Danny had established his credibility with me as an *Expert*. I was immediately very comfortable with the "opportunity" to hire him to work on my car.

My next words to Danny were, "Can we schedule this for Saturday morning?"

We went on, for many months, to have a great relationship. I never questioned any part he bought or repair he made. I trusted the guy.

He was so honest that at one time he told me my next repair would be more than the vehicle was worth. The 'Cash for Clunkers' program had just been initiated by the government, and, because of Danny's integrity, I jumped on it. (*Thank you*, fellow taxpayers!)

Isn't that a great story! Each time I tell it to audiences they **"GET IT!"** also. *Your* Elevator Speech should have that kind of effect on your audience, and lead to a sale, also.

21

Chapter 3 - My Elevator Speech

What follows is *my* Elevator Speech. It is the culmination of much research, testing, and tweaking. It is the one I deliver, when given the opportunity, in front of groups. It goes "from the ground floor to the top floor." Since it covers *everything* I want to tell a **group**, I refer to it as "The *Ultimate* Elevator Speech."

Please read it and "hear" my voice as you do.

Kindly read it a second *time* and consider how it might look in *your* world. Remember, I did much testing and tweaking when developing this, and finding the right wording for yours will not be done the first time you compose it. It's a *process,* not an *event!*

We'll then take a look at each "floor" and see how it was crafted. It's about thirty-seven seconds in length.

My "Ultimate Elevator Speech"

Hello. My name is Fred Miller.

I'm a speaker, a coach, and an author.

The title of my *first* book is, *"NO SWEAT* Public Speaking!"

Businesses, individuals, and organizations *hire* me *because* they want to improve their public speaking and presentation skills.

They do that because they know, *Speaking* Opportunities are *Business*, *Career*, and *Leadership* Opportunities.

They also know; we perceive *really good* speakers as *experts!* We *like* to work with *experts*.

I show them how to develop, practice, and deliver, a '*Knock your Socks Off!*' presentation with - **NO SWEAT!**

Note: I did not go to the eighth floor, but sometimes I do. (More on this floor in a bit.)

The Elevator Speech - Floor by Floor

Now that you've read it, what do you think?

My goal is that you know *exactly* what I do and my expertise for doing it. You can now make an educated decision:
➡ "File" for future use if needed for yourself or to refer.
➡ Refer to someone you could help.
➡ Have a conversation with me to learn more for yourself or people you know.
  • You may decide to *Hire* Me!

If you liked it, read on and I'll show you how it was crafted. If not, that's OK. Other people take different views on what an Elevator Speech should be, and you may prefer something else. You might also want to take bits and pieces of mine, customize it, and add something you think I've left out.

If mine struck a chord with you, continue and tweak it to match *your* world!

Let's get into the Elevator!

First Floor - Describe Who You Are

Hello! My name is Fred Miller

That may be all someone wants to know about you - **Your Name**.

Often, in the **One-on-one Situation**, they may just be being polite. If that's the case - fine.

Move on to someone you've *targeted* to meet (more on *targeting* in a future chapter), and initiate a conversation. *"Hi, Bob. I'm Fred Miller and I've looked forward to meeting you."* They'll probably respond, when shaking your hand, *"Pleased to meet you. What do you do?"* (Great! I'm taking Bob to the next floor!)

Some people have names that are difficult to pronounce. (Fred isn't one of them!) They can also be challenging, for those hearing them, to visualize. If that happens, the name can become a distraction, keeping the recipient(s) focused on the person's name. They might be trying to figure spelling, derivation, or ethnicity of it and they'll likely miss the next "floors."

When the last name is one that falls into this category, use your first name only when introducing yourself. You can give them your last name and other contact information later if your Elevator Speech leads to a future conversation.

If the first name is an odd or difficult one for people not familiar with it, pronounce it slowly, and, if useful, relate it to something they are familiar with.

Another solution is to say it without hurrying, spell it at a slow pace, and say it, again.

Second Floor - Describe What You Do

I'm a Speaker, a Coach, and an Author.

That's what I do. Those three descriptions are clear, succinct, and easily understood.

Sometimes people tell me they wear many hats and do many things. They have a hard time deciding what to say they do. Think about the tasks that make you money and you like doing. Use those and limit it to 'three'. (More on why 'three' is important later.)

With *both* the Group and One-on-one audiences, they might want to know more:
- ➡ *What* I speak about.
- ➡ *What* I coach.
- ➡ *What* I've written.

What describes *you?*
- ➡ Describe it *simply.*
  - "I'm an insurance rep."
  - "I'm a CPA."
    - Most people know CPA stands for Certified Public Accountant. However, other alphabet abbreviations may not be as well known and should be either followed by the words they stand for or eliminate the abbreviation.

- **Examples:**
  - EVP, Executive Vice-president.
  - CFO, Chief Financial Officer,
  - CMO, Chief Marketing Officer.
- ➡ "I'm a graphic designer."
- ➡ "I'm a patent attorney."
- ➡ I'm a doctor."

➡You *want* them to know what you do, and not feel ignorant they don't know what you're talking about.

➡People "see the emperor with no clothes, but don't say anything."

➡If it is a profession that may need some explanation, give that clarification after stating what it is.

- **Examples:**
  - "I'm a Ironmonger. That's someone who sells things made out of iron. My specialty is yard sculpture."
  - "I'm a pediatric hematologist/oncologist. I treat children and teens with blood diseases and cancer."

- You may think your profession doesn't need an explanation, but it might. Clarity is essential to a great Elevator Speech.

- **Example:** Everyone doesn't know what a **Sous Chef** is. (That individual is the second in command in a kitchen and reports to the head chef.)

Third Floor - Describe Your Expertise or Experience

The Title of My first Book is "NO SWEAT Public Speaking!"

If not pressed for time, I might include the subtitle: *"How to Develop, Practice, and Deliver a 'Knock Your Socks Off' Presentation with - **NO SWEAT!**"*

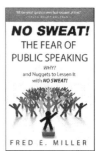

The perception of someone who wrote a book is they are an expert. That's one of the reasons I wrote several books, and why I mention it on the "Expertise Floor."

➡ If you haven't written a book, consider doing it!
  • It doesn't have to be the next "War and Peace."
  • A PDF available on your website makes you an author, doesn't it?
  • POD, Print-on-demand publishing makes the entire process easier than ever. Look into it at Createspace.com, LightningSource.com, Lulu.com and other self-publishing sites.

Other examples of Expertise are:
  • Years in business.
  • Industry awards.
  • Family owned, third generation.
  • Largest in area.
  • Academic degrees.
  • Published papers, articles, and books.
  • News articles about the individual or company.
  • Patents and copyrights.
  • Only one of its kind.

Titles can convey expertise and prestige, a good quality to have!

Examples:
- Owner.
- President.
- VP of Sales.
- Proprietor.
- Innkeeper.
- Charge Nurse.
- General Manager.
- Managing Partner.
- Chief Resident.

Note: A person's Title can be used with the second floor, as in:
- I'm the Owner of City Hardware.
- I'm the VP of Sales for Computer Hardware and Repair Service.
- I'm the Head Librarian.

This floor is important because it lends **credibility** to your Elevator Speech. Get help with this. Often, we're "too close to ourselves and *don't know what we know.*" Have people who know you well, tell you what your expertise is. You might be surprised!

Fourth Floor - Why They Hire Me

Business, Individuals, and Organizations Hire Me Because They want to Improve Their Public Speaking and Presentation Skills.

"Hire me," is the phrase my classmate, Roy Reichold, used that resulted in *everyone* in class, writing those words on a piece of paper and incorporating them into

their elevator speeches. Those two words pushed me into researching Elevator Speeches and writing this book.

"Hire me," grabs our attention, *doesn't it?*

I prefer the words *Hire Me* instead of. . .
"I *work* with people who. . .
"I *help* companies. . .

Hire Me says,
—I'm *Proud* of what I do.
Hire Me says,
—I'm *Good* at what I do.
Hire Me makes it clear,
—I *"don't do this for free!"*

Hire Me can be an excellent *Dis*-Qualifier, especially with the One-On-One Audience.

> If *Hire Me* turns them off - *fine!*
> Move on to someone who might "want to know more," and appreciates the message, *"Hire Me,"* implies.

During the Q&A segment of one of my Elevator Speech Presentations, one attendee commented she thought my *"Hire Me"* phrase had an *"Attitude"* attached to it. I *agreed* and replied it was a *good* Attitude! Would you rather deal with someone who is wishy-washy about their expertise, services, and products? *Not me!*

If you don't like the phrase, *"Hire Me,"* try one of these:
- Businesses and individuals *pay* me to. . .
- Businesses *put me on their payroll* to. . .
- People *give me money* to. . .
- Companies *invest* in my expertise to. . .
- Individuals *spend money* with me to. . .

Depending on your profession, one of the following could fit:
- People become *my patients.* . .
- Individuals and companies *become our clients.* . .
- Home owners *have their major appliances serviced by us.* . .

An individual delivering an Elevator Speech for their company might say. . .
- Companies *become our customers.* . .
- Home owners *hire our company.* . .
- Local governments *engage our service*s. . .

Non-Profits might say. . .
- People *write us checks.* . .
- Individuals *give us money.* . .
- Companies *donate* to us. . .
- Service clubs *volunteer* for us. . .

The word, *"Because"* is important in this floor of the Elevator Speech. It is an "Influencer Word" that affects recipients about what the speaker is saying.

Dr. Robert Cialdini, in his famous book, "Influence," points out this word has a unique motivational influence.

Do you remember something like this from your childhood?

> "Why do I have to do that, mom?"
> *"Because* I said so!"

Other examples:
- *Because* it's the right thing to do.
- *Because* we have to.

Use the word *"Because"* in your Elevator Speech *because* it makes a difference!

Fifth Floor - Your *WHY*

They Know:
Speaking Opportunities are Business, Career, and Leadership Opportunities.

Sometimes I add, "That's my mantra! *No one* ever challenges that statement. *Why would they!"*

I *could* follow this up with,
"Are you *taking* and *making* Speaking Opportunities?" That could continue the conversation. This is an Elevator Speech, *not* a sales presentation. If this leads to a meeting and a conversation, I'll ask it then.

The **Fifth Floor** is *beyond* important. **It is the DNA of your Elevator Speech**. It is the center of *WHY* you do what you do and derived from Simon Sinek's TED Talk, "How great leaders inspire action." He talks about the Golden Circle; three concentric Circles with *WHY* in the middle, **How**, next and **WHAT** on the outside. Simon gives reasons you should start with *WHY*. It's central *to* **What** you do! Here's the URL: http://goo.gl/uTUOeg

SIMON SINEK'S
GOLDEN CIRCLE

Your WHY is the DNA
of your Elevator Speech.

I won't go through his entire presentation, but essentially, his message is: People don't buy **WHAT** you do; They buy *WHY* you do it.

Simon says most companies start with **WHAT**.
Example:
> "We're a big computer company, and we make great computers with lots of ram and memory, and they are inexpensive. Want to buy one?"
> (Not a message that grabs me!)

A few firms, like Apple, **GET IT!** and start with *WHY*.
Example:

> "Do you want to be creative?"

Do you want to be more productive than you could ever imagine and do you want   to do it with equipment that's fun and easy to use?
We're Apple!"
(Yes!)

My **WHY**, as stated on the fifth floor is:
"They *Know: Speaking* Opportunities are *Business, Career*, and *Leadership* Opportunities."
If you don't believe that statement, you don't need or want, what I offer.

The Goal is not to do business with everybody who needs what you have.

The Goal is to do business with
people who believe what you believe.

—Simon Sinek

Simon says:
➡ **WHY** - is not profit. Profit is a result.
➡ He asks:
   • What's your purpose?
   • What's your cause?
   • What's your belief?
   • Why do you exist?
   • Why do you get up in the morning?

WHY Examples:

> "They *know* one of the best uses of their charitable contributions is *teaching* people to better their *own* lives."

> "They *know* saving the lives of young children is a *far* better feeling than being super rich."

Watch his video several times and use Simon Sinek's teachings to find *your* **WHY!**

Sixth Floor - More *Why* They Hire Me

They also know...

We Perceive Really Good Speakers as Experts. We Like to Work with Experts.

Audiences agree with this statement *because* it makes sense, doesn't it?

Examples from other Elevator Speeches are:
- They do this b*ecause* they want it done right the *first* time.
- They do this b*ecause* their business success *depends* on it.
- They do this b*ecause* *quality* and *safety* are their main concerns.

For a Nonprofit:
- They do this *because* their dollars go to a cause that *really* makes a difference in people's lives.
- They do this *because* the results of their volunteer work are *immediately* apparent, appreciated, and humbling.

Increase *your* credibility on the Sixth Floor *because* it matters!

Seventh Floor - I Deliver

I Show Them How to Develop, Practice, and Deliver a 'Knock Your Socks Off!' Presentation with - NO SWEAT!

This sentence tells very clearly what an individual or company will gain by *hiring me.*

What does your product or service do that makes *hiring you* a good decision? What problem do you solve? **What benefit** will they realize by spending money with your company?

The *"NO SWEAT"* verbiage is part of my **Personal Branding**. If you have a "Brand," this is a great place to use it!

Here's why:
One of the Rules of Public Speaking/Presenting is the "Law of Primacy and Recency."

The Law of Primacy and Recency says: "The *last* thing you say and do, will be the *first* thing the audience will remember.

It says, we best remember the *first* and *last* things we see and hear in a presentation. Since an Elevator Speech is a mini-presentation, this law applies. The *last* thing they hear will be the *first* thing they'll remember. *"NO SWEAT"* is something they'll recall long after we part ways.

If you don't have a personal brand, seriously consider developing one. I have several Posts on Personal Branding starting here:

http://www.nosweatpublicspeaking.com/no-sweat-branding/

Examples from other Elevator Speeches are:
- "I file all their tax related transactions on time, with the correct taxing entity, and make certain all available discounts are taken."
- "We *guarantee* the job will be completed on time, within budget, with no defects."

For a Nonprofit:
- "We make certain the skills and enthusiasm they bring as a volunteer is maximized for themselves and those they serve."

- "We put their contribution to work in the donor's specifically designated area and provide full transparency. That's why so many regularly write us checks!"

Eighth Floor - Ask!

This floor is only used in one-on-one Elevator Speech situations. If you've taken the individual to this floor, there should be some interest in what you do.

The usual question people pose is, "What do you do?"

It's OK to do that, but asking in a different manner can help you prospect.

Example:
"You probably don't know any company or person who needs the kind of services I provide - do you?"

Questioning, in this manner, will catch them a bit off guard. It usually gets them thinking about someone who might be a prospect; maybe themselves!

Their answer could lead to a sale!

Or

"*Enough about me.* How does *your* company handle internal and external presentation training?"

Asking, "Do you, or anyone you know, need what I offer?" is *not* a good way to ask. It requires a "Yes" or "No" answer. It will usually be "No'" and the conversation is over!

Examples from other Elevator Speeches are:

- "You probably never have any late tax filings, *do you?*"
- "The work flow at your company is about as good as it gets, *isn't it?*"

For a Nonprofit:
- "How does your company decide where their people's volunteer efforts should be steered?"
- "What criteria do you look at before making a donation?"

Skipping Floors

Often, with both the Group and the Individual, Face-to-face Audiences, there are **time constraints.**

Skipping floors, when necessary, is easy to do when the Elevator Speech is built Floor by Floor. (You don't stop at every floor when going to the penthouse, do you?) **Example:** When I'm given "ten-seconds or less to give an Elevator Speech."

"I'm Fred Miller. I'm a Speaker, Coach, and an Author. Businesses, Individuals, and Organizations, *hire me* to improve their Public Speaking and Presentation Skills."

Whether given ten, fifteen, thirty-seconds or a minute, I can fill the time with a varying number of "Floors."

The "Twitter® Type" Elevator Speech

Sometimes, because there is a large group or tight time constraints, the leader says, "Please deliver your Elevator Speech in *twenty words or less*."

This can be a challenge, but well worth the effort.

As in most editing activities, *less* is *more*. Twitter has made us do that. (One huge downside is the growing use of abbreviations it has spawned. These hurt the communication skills of many when they try to communicate "normally" but are still in "Twitter Mode.")

Here's my "Twitter Type" Elevator Speech:
"I write, speak, and coach about Public Speaking and Presentation Skills."

18 Words
83 Characters

I like that sentence so much, I sometimes use it as my *first* floor when going up!

Chapter 4 - The Elevator Speech - Delivering It

Every presentation, including an Elevator Speech, has **Two Components**.

1. **Content**
   - The Message you want the audience to **GET!**
     - Here, it is the *information* on each "Floor" of the Elevator Speech.
2. **Delivery**
   - Presenting that Message.
     - Setting forth the floors of the Elevator Speech.

In all presentations, from Elevator Speech to Keynote Presentation: *Delivery trumps Content!*

A person's Elevator Speech might have great content on each floor, but if not delivered properly, the results will not meet the intended goals.

The **Delivery Component** of a Presentation has **Two Parts**.

1. **Verbal**
   - Your voice and how you use it.
     - It's not just *what* you say, but *how* you say it.
2. **Nonverbal**
   - Almost everything except your voice.

In all presentations, *Nonverbal trumps Verbal Delivery.* We believe what we see!

Note this - Remember this - Practice this!

Don't Be Mechanical in Your Delivery
Many of us have heard an Elevator Speech delivered as if it were prerecorded. It's almost as though the presenter pressed a switch that started an audio file playing.

The message is often delivered too quickly to be understood and in a monotone, boring manner. If there were an On/Off Switch, you'd be searching for it and others would cheer when you turned it off.

You should "struggle" a bit when you give an Elevator Speech. More on this aspect of delivery when we look at "Practicing."

Verbal Communication

The elements of Verbal Communication are:

1. Enunciation and Pronunciation

a. If the audience, individual or group, can't decipher what you are saying, they'll never **GET IT!**
b. Talk so people understand the words you are speaking. *Don't mumble or slur your language!*

      i. Words must be pronounced distinctly and correctly, or they won't be understood.

  c. People with regional and foreign accents often need to work on this more than others.

      i. A strong Southern drawl or robust New Jersey accent could lose an audience if not native to those areas.

2. Inflection

a. Don't be a Star Wars' R2D2 character and speak in monotone because it can be very boring and hard to understand.

      i. Some cultures speak in a more monotone manner than others and need to work on this speaking element more than those from a very expressive heritage.

b. Inflecting *specific words* can *dramatically* change the meaning of what you say.

      i. By contrast, stressing the wrong words will not make the points you intend to convey.

c. Decide which words in your Elevator Speech are the most important and emphasize them when delivering. Practice stressing different words and hear the difference!

d. **Example**: (The *italicized* words should be emphasized.)

      i. Read *without* emphasizing any words; then read it with the indicated emphasis. You'll agree it's an *amazing* difference.)

         1. "*Speaking* Opportunities are *Business*, *Career*, and *Leadership* Opportunities!"

That's *my mantra. No one ever* challenges that statement. *Why would they?*

3. Cadence

a. Speak **too quickly** and they won't **GET IT!**
   i. My experience, from listening to many Elevator Speeches, is most people speak *way too quickly* when delivering their talk, especially in the Group Scenario. Many do this because of the Fear of Public Speaking. Others, because they don't realize how much time they really have to deliver. Often, the allotted time is thirty-seconds, and the speaker completes it in fifteen! The result is the audience *doesn't* **GET IT!**
b. Speak **too slowly** and you'll lose them.
c. *Vary* the cadence and you'll do a better job of keeping their attention.
d. **Practice and Time yourself.** Thirty-seconds is longer than most think it is.
   i. Use a stop watch and time yourself starting with three floors and adding floors to see how much time you really have. (*My* ultimate Elevator Speech is only 37 seconds long.)

4. Pausing

a. Silence is tough for most of us. We want to fill the silence with sound, and we usually do it with our voice.
b. Pausing is possibly the most important element of the Verbal Communication. It gives the recipient or

audience time to absorb and process what you've said.

    i. They have to process and understand your message if they're to understand it.

c. If you've used humor and people are laughing, pause, and don't talk over their laughter. Talk over their laughter and they'll miss part of your message.

d. Plan your pauses to emphasize something important you want them to know.

    i. **Example**: (The *italicized* words should be emphasized and PAUSE where indicated.)

        1. *"Speaking* Opportunities are *Business, Career,* and *Leadership* Opportunities!"* (PAUSE)

"People who *take* and *make* those *Speaking* Opportunities (PAUSE), *grow* their Businesses, *advance* their careers, and *increase* their Leadership Roles.

Nonverbal Communication

Have you ever seen a professional Mime perform? They are amazing! With no words, you know *exactly* the message they are communicating. That's the power of Nonverbal Communication.

Nonverbal Communication falls into Two Categories:

    1. **Voluntary**, those we do consciously.

    2. **Involuntary**, those we do unconsciously.

The audience doesn't care which it is. The **visuals** they *see* you deliver will overrule the words they *hear.*
i.e. We believe what we see!

Voluntary Nonverbal Communication

Use Nonverbal Communication to reinforce the words you speak and enhance your presentation. These are the **Elements of Nonverbal Communication.**

1. Eye Contact

1. "The eyes are the gateway to the soul," is a phrase many are familiar with. It means our eyes are a very expressive part of our face and much can be derived about a person by looking at them.
   a. Our eyes can "twinkle" and "smile!"
   b. Make **eye contact** with people you are speaking with.
      i. It conveys honesty and sincerity.
      ii. It shows a *confidence* in your *competence.*
      iii. Survey the audience until you see someone who is **Getting** your message. Look them in the eye - finish a thought - move on to someone else who gives you great feedback.

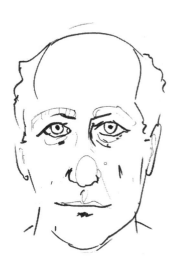

      1. *Don't* be a "searchlight" beacon; moving your head, mechanically, side to side scanning the audience.
      iv. *Not* looking people in the eye makes them wary of your honestly. (There are, however, some cultural exceptions, notably: Native

American, most Latin-American, Asian, and African societies.)

 v. Don't stare!

  1. Most of us get uncomfortable if someone is staring at us.

  2. You're not connecting with most of your audience if you're staring at one individual.

2. Facial Expressions

a. Smile!

 i. Smiling is universally understood. It warms people to you.

 ii. Smiling is *contagious.*

  1. I refer to a smile as being a "Nonphysical Hug:"

   a. When you give one, you usually get one right back!

 iii. Other **Facial Expressions** are also universal and "seen" the same by people all over the globe. They include expressions for:

  1. Fear, Anger, Surprise, Disgust, Happiness, and being Sad.

3. Gestures

a. Surely you've seen, or maybe you are, someone who "talks with their hands."
   i. It's something, to one degree, or another, we naturally do, especially when we feel strongly about the subject we are talking about.
b. These include not just movements made with hands and arms, but also the legs, shoulders, and other body parts.
   i. **Examples**:
      1. "I'm going to *kick* the troublemakers out of class!"
      2. "Jeez! (While slapping yourself in the forehead.) I should have known the answer to *that* question!"
c. Exaggerate them for large audiences.
d. Be certain they are in sync with your message.

4. Body Language

a. **Posture**: straight with shoulders back and chest out shows "confidence in your competence."
b. Don't slouch, lean, or fidget when standing.
c. Don't put your hands in your pockets.
   i. Suggestion: If you're prone to fiddle with things in pockets, remove keys, change, and other items from your pants pockets.
d. NO Fig Leaf, Parade Rest, or Superman Stances!
   i. Be "Natural" in your posture.
e. Posture also applies when sitting, *before* and *after* you speak.
   i. Consider yourself *always* "on stage."
   ii. If, while waiting your turn to give your Elevator Speech, you are slouching or checking email on your smartphone, you're not sending the right message to others.
      1. Look at the person who is speaking.

5. Body Movement

   i. Consider yourself *always* "on stage" here, also.
   ii. Movements should be intentional and deliberate.
  iii. Don't "ping pong" yourself from one spot in the room to another. (For an Elevator Speech, you should be standing in one place.)

6. Clothing

a. What you wear should not distracting. It should be proper and suitable for the occasion and audience.
   i. Bling, ostentatious clothing, and flashy jewelry, should be avoided because they often draw away from your message.

Involuntary Nonverbal Communication

Some of the elements below can be considered *Voluntary*, and they *are* if done on purpose. If not deliberately made, and done in sync with the speaker's voice and words, they can give the audience a mixed message. *People believe what they see.*

Example:
I could say, "I'm really enjoying meeting you and other interesting people at this event!" However, if I yawn, look at my watch, and don't show enthusiasm in my gestures and expressions, what will you believe?

Examples of Nonverbal Communication include:
➡ Facial Expressions
   • Yawning, laughing, frowning, raised eyebrows, wincing, etc.

➡ Gestures
- Fidgeting, scratching, and gestures not in sync with message.

➡ Body Language
- Slouching, leaning, and more.

➡ Body Movement
- Random and distracting.

➡ Clothing
- Stained, wrinkled, missing buttons, etc.

Sometimes Involuntary Communication can give a message we didn't intend to deliver. Our audience might "see" us as disinterested, bored, speaking out of both sides of our mouth, and worse.

It's imperative to be aware of what our Non-verbal Communication is "telling" people. *Knowing* all components, parts, and elements of a presentation must be in sync, and mindful of the fact our Involuntary Non-verbal Communication could torpedo our message, will make us better speakers.

Do you "See" what I mean?

Sometimes *Involuntary*
NonVerbal Communication can give a
message we didn't intend to deliver.

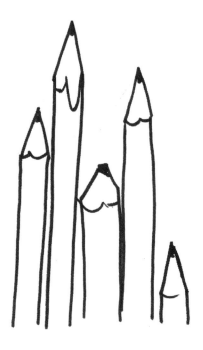

Chapter 5 - Bonus Tips for a Great Elevator Speech

1. Shake Hands!

A good firm handshake, held for a moment longer than normal, conveys a good message. It says, "I really care about meeting you and making a connection." A perfunctory one tells the recipient the opposite.

Both "Fish Handshakes" and "Bone Crushers" are absolutely unacceptable. You leave the recipient wanting to get away and never return!

2. Take the Temperature of Your Audience

When you're giving your Elevator Speech, you're the only one speaking, but you're getting feedback from those watching and listening to you.

Look for eye contact, facial expressions, and body language. These nonverbal communication elements will tell you whether the audience is **GETTING IT!**

If the feedback you observe tells you they are confused by what you are saying, take it to heart and rewrite that specific part of your Elevator Speech.

3. Interact with Your Audience

Interacting engages the people you are speaking with increasing the odds they'll **GET IT!**

Here are some ways to do that:
Ask questions. This activity engages people because you're not just delivering information, you are *asking* for them to think about what you asked and respond.

Example from my Elevator Speech:
"We perceive really good speakers as *Experts*. We like to work with Experts, *don't we?"*
The words, *"Don't we?"* elicit a response, *doesn't it!* The response could be a verbal, "yes!" or nonverbal affirmative head nodding.

Get a physical interaction:
Example from one of my Elevator Speech presentations.
"Raise your hand if you've changed, tweaked, or trashed your Elevator Speech in the last year!" (As I speak those words, I raise my hand high. Raising *my* hand high, gets

more people raising *their* hands, than merely asking the question without raising my hand.)

4. Buzz Words

Every industry has buzz words, acronyms, and techno-speak. Because they, and their colleges always use them, they think everyone knows their meaning. They do not. *Don't use them!*

You do not impress people by speaking language they don't understand. *You lose them!*

Example:
One of the groups I work with is financial advisors. They'll talk to folks about, "ETFs, mutual funds, derivatives, etc." Their audiences, composed of prospects, and clients, are shaking their heads up and down as if they understand those terms. *Most of them don't!* No one likes to feel stupid. We see the emperor with no clothes, but no one says anything.

Use simple language in your Elevator Speech. You want them to **GET IT!**

5. The Rule of Three

We're all familiar with famous 'Threes.'

- "Three strikes you're out!"
- "The third time is the charm."
- The Three Little Pigs.

Using 'Three' in your Elevator Speech can be *Magic!*

In his book, *Writing Tools: 50 Essential Strategies for Every Writer,* Roy Peter Clark provides insights to the magic of the number three. He says the following:

➡ Use **One** for emphasis.
  - "*This* is a great place to hold a convention!"
➡ Use **Two** for comparison.
  - Hot - Cold
  - High - Low
➡ Use **Three** for Completeness.
  - (Examples to follow.)
➡ Use **Four** or more for a list.
  - Grocery shopping list.
  - School supplies needed.

Examples from my Elevator Speech of the Magic of the Rule of Three.
- "I'm a Speaker, Coach and an Author."
- "*Speaking* Opportunities are *Business, Career,* and *Leadership* Opportunities."
- "*Businesses, Individuals,* and *Organizations* hire because they want to improve their Public Speaking and Presentation Skills."
- "I *Speak, Coach,* and *Write* about Public Speaking and Presentation Skills."

Three items are *Magic* in an Elevator Speech and all Presentations. We often use three things intuitively. Now that you aware of the Power of Three, you'll consciously add an item to two you're using, and reduce to three if parts of your presentation are four or more points.

6. Tag Line

- "If it's Sunday, it's Meet the Press." - NBC Sunday morning magazine show.
- "I will see *you* at the top." - Zig Ziglar
- "You're in good hands with Allstate." - Allstate Insurance Company
- "Don't leave home without it." - American Express
- "I'm Lovin' It!" - McDonalds

I'll bet some of the above tag lines are familiar to you. You probably knew whom they belong to without the owner being named.

Ideally, your Elevator Speech will have a Tag Line because Tag Lines are remembered. If they relate to whom you are and what you do, so much the better. Recalling you, and your products and services, is a goal of a great Elevator Speech!

Example
I end all my Elevator Speeches and Presentations with,
". . .absolutely, positively; there's no doubt in my mind; no
ifs, ands, or doubts about it. *Your* Elevator Speech
(Presentation) *will* be - **NO SWEAT!**"
If I'm speaking with folks who've heard me before, many
will, as I do when closing my presentation, wipe their
brow and say the words - **NO SWEAT!**

How cool is that!

7. "Quotable Quote"

How great would it be to have others quote you? *Super*
great is the correct answer.

A "Quotable Quote" is similar to a Tag Line. In fact, it
could be your Tag Line. It is something you've said that
has substance, is memorable, and is easy for others to
say.

It must be relevant to the content of your message and
something you want others to take to heart and believe.
Ideally, it should be one sentence; i.e. "Less is More."

"Less is more."

This "Quotable Quote" is often associated with the
architect and furniture designer Ludwig Mies Van Der
Rohe (1886-1969), one of the founders of modern
architecture and a proponent of simplicity of style.

Other "Quotable Quotes" and their authors are:
- "Love the life you live, live the life you love." - Bob
  Marley
- "Never, never, never give up." —Winston Churchill

- "Failure is the opportunity to begin again, more intelligently." - Henry Ford
- "We may have all come on different ships, but we're in the same boat now." - Martin Luther King

My "Quotable Quote," from *my* elevator Speech, is:

"***Speaking*** **Opportunities are** ***Business, Career,*** **and** ***Leadership*** **Opportunities!"**

For that quote to have more impact I'll add, "That's *my mantra.* No one *ever* challenges that statement. *Why would they!"*

Think about what you offer and what you want the audience to take away from your Elevator Speech. Experiment with different "Quotable Quotes." Eventually, you'll come up with something that others will be saying and telling where they heard it!

8. Props

Your audience has three learning styles.
I.   Visual
    1. 65% of the population learns by looking at something, usually something other than text.
      a) "I see what you mean."
II.   Auditory
    A. 35% of audiences learn best by listening.
      1. "I hear what you're saying."
III. Kinesthetic
    A. 5% of us learn by doing.

Appealing to two or more of those learning styles increases the odds your audience will **GET IT!**

Props appeal to the visual learners. "Showing" what you do can dramatically and instantly increase understanding of what you do.

Examples:
- A doctor might hold a stethoscope in the air.
- A glassblower shows his beautiful wares to the audience.
- Financial planners can hold wads of cash in their hand for people to see.

I'm sure the above helped you "see" what I mean.

Caveats for Props:
→ They must be relevant to what you do.
→ Show them, if necessary, briefly explain them, then put them out of sight.
- Unless you do, they could become a distraction. People will be looking at the prop, and not listening to you. We cannot multitask!

9. Conversational

Keep your Elevator Speech conversational.

Your brief talk is not a sermon or a lecture. You should speak as you normally talk. A great speech should be like a one-on-one conversation.

You never want to be too smooth when delivering any presentation. It's not a good way to relate to people. Struggling, and sometimes stumbling, is human. Those are frailties we can all relate too.

This takes practice. More on this later.

10. Find a Friendly Face

When delivering your Elevator
Speech to a group, there are
individuals who are paying
attention to what you are
saying and understanding your
message. These people are
genuinely interested in your
message.

They are looking at you and
giving positive feedback. Find
one of those people and make
eye contact. Finish speaking a
thought, and move on to reach
another friendly face. Finish
speaking another thought, and
repeat.

Those individuals are important. They'll give you energy,
increase the quality of your speech, and decrease your
anxiety.

If you see an unfriendly face - move on to someone else!

Don't take the look on those unpleasant faces personally.
People bring all kinds of baggage to meetings, and your
Elevator Speech can be the last thing on their mind.

When delivering your Elevator Speech, *you* are the only one speaking, but the audience *is* communicating with you.

Chapter 6 - Tips for Networking

Networking Goals

Unfortunately, many go to a networking event, walk into the room, look for people they know, and spend the majority of the event with them. *That's not networking!*

Others, upon entering the same room, strike up a conversation with someone new, and spend the entire period with them. *That's not networking!*

Networking is the opportunity to use your Elevator Speech as a *Dis*qualifying tool. You don't want to go to the "top floor" with everyone. Our **goal** is twofold:

1. They stop you at one of the "floors" and say, "I have an interest! Let's get on each other's calendars next week and continue this conversation. Here's my card, please give me yours."

2. They *Dis*qualify themselves by indicating there is no interest in what you do, and not immediately coming up with the name of someone they know you should have a conversation with.
Move on to someone else!

63

Functions, Meetings, and Seminars don't have to be formally called a Networking Event to do networking.

These gatherings are great for meeting people who are prospects, or know prospects, for your products and services.

They are also great for meeting people for things that can benefit you and people you know.

Another goal of going to a Networking Event is to meet folks are great *Connectors.* These are people who seem to know *everyone.* (You've seen these people, haven't you!) If they *don't* know someone, they probably know someone who does. Since an introduction to someone is usually more valuable than introducing yourself, you'll want to include these people on your "must meet" list.

Before the Event - Make a Plan

I. Do some research.
    A. Often, the attendee's name, company, and sometimes, position, is listed on the event's home page.
        1. Meetup.com and Eventbrite.com, an event on-line registration service, do this! Check them out when they are used by the event organizer.
II. When you find out who is attending, target and prioritize a list of the people you want to meet.
    A. Look them up on LinkedIn.
        1. You might find someone *you* know, who *knows* the person you want to meet, and *will* be attending the function.
            a) Contact your connection and ask whether they'd be willing to introduce you to your target.

b) Even if your connection isn't attending, you now know you know someone they know (are you following this?) Use that commonality as part of your conversation when meeting your target.
B. Look them up on FaceBook and follow the above suggestions for LinkedIn.
C. *Google* your target's name. You'll be *amazed* at what you might find out that could be common grounds for a conversation.

At the Event - Work Your Plan

I. First things first!
A. Your list of people to cont act is prioritized - *work it that way!*

1. You may not meet as *many* people if done another way, like talking to the first person you see, but you'll meet the ones considered the most important for reaching your objective.
2. Find those people!
    a) If they are engaged in a conversation with someone, *don't* interrupt. Make eye contact so they know you want to introduce yourself.
    b) If they are speaking with someone, and it seems as though it will go on for a while, seek out the next person on your list.

II. Use your Elevator Speech to *dis*qualify people. Find those who have an interest and want to continue the conversation, in depth, later.

III. *Give* business cards and *get* them.

   A. Write short notes of the encounter on the back of their card so you can recall key points of the conversation and what, if anything, is the next step.

Have a Getaway Plan

The time to meet new people is limited, and one goal is *not* to spend *major* time on *minor* possibilities. Have a plan to get away from folks when they are *dis*qualified.

Suggestion:
When you realize the conversation isn't with a prospect or someone who will be referring you, say, "Excuse me. I've set a goal for this event to meet ten people I haven't met before. You're number _____ . Let's continue this conversation another time." Write a note on the back of their business card, shake their hand, and find the next person on your target list.

Delivering the Elevator Speech at a Networking Event, One-on-One

What follows is a typical scenario for meeting a person at the networking portion of an event.

I approach the person I want to meet, extend my hand, give a firm grasp, shake their hand and say.

"Hi!
My name is Fred Miller."

They will respond with their name, and might say, "Nice to meet you, Fred. What do you do?"

I respond,
    "I'm a speaker, a coach, and an author."

The response might be,
    "Oh! What have you written?"

I answer.
    "The title of my first book is, *"NO SWEAT* Public Speaking!"

They continue the conversation and say,
    "Interesting. Tell me more.*"

Since they've shown an interest, I go to the next floor of my Elevator Speech and say,

    "Businesses, individuals, and organizations *hire* me *because* they want to improve their public speaking and presentation skills.

If they continue to show an interest, verbally or nonverbally, I continue,

> "They do that because they *know*: *Speaking* Opportunities are *Business*, *Career*, and *Leadership* Opportunities.

As long as they're still showing interest and haven't stopped me, I'll go to the next floor.

> "They also know we perceive *really good speakers* as *Experts!* We like to work with Experts - right?"

Since they are still "on the elevator," I tell them What I Deliver by saying.

> *"I* show them how to develop, practice, and deliver, a '*knock your socks off!'* presentation with - *NO SWEAT!"*

In this scenario, I go on to the 8th Floor where I ASK,

> "Enough about me. How does *your* company handle internal and external Presentation Skill Training?"

Have a *Post* Network Event Plan

➡ Have a *debriefing with yourself* on how your networking efforts went.
  - What did you do well?
  - What can you improve?
➡ How many targeted people you met and what the next steps are.
  - If the next step for some is to get on each other's calendars - *do it sooner rather than later.*

- The next day is a good time to followup.
- It may require a phone call or email that has more information with links that will inform the person more about what you do.

➡ Enter all the contact information and post-contact information into your CRM software.

Networking is the opportunity to use your Elevator Speech as a *Dis*qualifying tool.

Chapter 7 - The Fear of Public Speaking

One of the main reasons people do a terrible job crafting and delivering Elevator Speeches is the Fear of Public Speaking.

Survey after survey indicates it is one of the most common fears people have. Up to 75% of the population, to one degree or another, has this fear. Some fear it more than dying! There's even a word for it - glossophobia. Glōssa, meaning tongue, comes from the Greek language. Phobos is fear. The important thing to note is glossophobia is a word, not a disease, and it can be lessened!

In my research, I've discovered the Fear of Public Speaking is an Equal Opportunity Fear. It doesn't care about your age, education or occupation. I have coached doctors, lawyers, students, entrepreneurs, psychologists, and many others.

Most of the keynote talks I give, workshops I conduct, or coaching I do, include a discussion about this fear. It holds many back, personally and professionally. In this section, I'll cover:
1. Why We have a Fear of Public Speaking.
2. Nuggets to Lessen that Fear.

WHY the Fear of Public Speaking?

Whenever I'm asked this, my first response is, *"Why not?"*

Think about it. Most our communication is one-on-one. Many of those conversations are via phone. We don't see the person.

Increasingly, communication is conducted by texting and email. We don't see or hear the other person.

It's normal, when standing in front of twenty, thirty, or more sets of eyeballs, to be uncomfortable. It's because we're "Out of our Comfort Zone."

That uncomfortableness will ease by speaking often and regularly; i.e. *widening* your comfort zone.

There are, however, several genuine reasons to have that fear.
- ➡ **If you don't know your topic.**
  - Don't get in front of an audience and speak about something you are not well versed in.
  - You'll never know everything about your subject, but should know enough that you're comfortable delivering the information to others, including people who are knowledgable of the subject matter.

- ➡ **If you don't know the structure of a presentation.**
  - We've all experienced a speaker who talked, talked, talked, didn't say much and was almost impossible to follow.
  - Don't be one of those speakers!

- Like a great cake, there is a recipe for developing and delivering a great Elevator Speech or Presentation.
    - You can learn that!
➡ **If you haven't practiced.**
- Practicing is not optional.

Additionally, there are situations where the Fear of Public Speaking can take hold.
➡ **Number of people in the audience.**
- Maybe it's no problem talking with three, five, or even ten people. Beyond that, it's dicey for some of us.
- An analogy is the Fear of Heights.
    - I don't mind getting on a stool, step stool, or step ladder. One that reaches the gutters above the second floor of my house - *not for me!*
➡ **Specific individuals in the audience.**
- Maybe it's not a problem speaking with a large audience, but if someone's boss, or colleagues are seated - *Yikes!*
➡ **Having to ask the audience to do something.**
- Maybe there's no anxiety speaking with a room full of people but if having to ask for something; maybe writing a check, or taking a pledge, nervousness can increase.

There are a couple important things I want to focus on before I *name* and *explain* the Nuggets to Lessen the Fear of Public Speaking.

Nervousness

Those **butterflies we feel in our stomach** from the Fear of Public Speaking; we *don't* want to get rid of them completely. We want to channel that energy into our

Elevator Speech. A presentation without energy is b-o-r-i-n-g! (Ever sit through one? *Yech!*)

Toastmasters says we should, "Teach those butterflies to fly in formation!" That's great advice.

Being **Audience Centered** is one of the **Laws of Presentation**.
It applies to Elevator Speeches, also.

Audience Centered

Successful businesses are *Customer Centered.* They focus on their customer's wants and needs. This means:
- Medicine is *Patient Centered.*
- Education is *Student Centered.*
- The Hospitality Industry is *Guest Centered.*

If we want to be successful in presenting our Elevator Speeches, we need to be ***Audience Centered.***

It's all about the Audience, not the speaker!

If *you* are the speaker, and I assume this is why you're reading this - It's *not about you!*

No one came to see and hear *you!* They came to learn something from the speaker at the event, the seminar you're all attending, and to network with others. *You* are *not* the reason they are attending.

If you take your focus off the audience and put it on yourself, you're in trouble - *Big Trouble!* You then start thinking about *you* and *your* presentation:
- "How do I look?"
- "Was I talking too quickly?"
- "Was I speaking too slowly?"
- "Rats! I think I forgot something."

Being **Audience Centered** is one of the **Laws of Presentation**, and applies to Elevator Speeches, also. Understand it, believe it, and practice it. The quality of your presentations will go *up*, and your anxiety will go *down!*

Speaking of the Audience, they're *cheering* for you! No one wants another to embarrass themselves with their

Elevator Speech. They *want* you to be successful in your delivery and find out what you do.

No one is looking for you to 'mess up' so they can dis you on your Facebook page!

If you do make a mistake, and show it non-verbally or tell them, they share your embarrassment, but don't think any less of you. *You* made the effort, *didn't you!*

Focus on the Audience, *not* on yourself.

Important Note:
All audiences are not the same!

What you said that got a great laughter from one group may find another collection of folks sitting stone-faced. That's the way it is, and you'll never know till you present your Elevator Speech.

Knowing this fact prepares you for those audiences. Expect it because it *will* happen.
Don't take it personally! Prepare and do the best you can for each audience, staying focused on *them.*

Chapter 8 - Nuggets to Lessen the Fear of Public Speaking

1. Never Tell Anyone You are Afraid!

I've seen individuals, when it's their turn to give their Elevator Speech, stand up and promptly announce, "I'm afraid of public speaking, hate doing this sort of thing, and didn't prepare."

Don't do that! Even if any of it is true - keep it to yourself! It could become a self-fulfilling prophecy.

If you make an announcement like that, the audience will be looking for something negative. With that kind of pressure, you probably won't disappoint them!

2. Arrive at the Event Early so You can Meet & Greet.

It is amazing how much easier it is to talk to an audience where you have already met the individuals who compose it.

Just introducing yourself, with an outstretched hand, and telling them, "I'm Fred. I'm glad you're here!" makes a huge difference in your anxiety level.

I am usually one of the first to arrive at an event. I want to greet as many people as possible. Other attendees appreciate your introduction and feel a connection to you.

3. Take the Temperature of the Audience

When delivering your Elevator Speech you are the only one speaking, but the audience *is* communicating with you. Their facial expressions and body language let you know if they are **GETTING IT!**

If there is confusion on their face, they're not, and you'll have to revisit the content and delivery of your Elevator Speech.

Make eye contact with your audience. It shows "confidence in your competence, and honesty." You'll be able to judge the reception of your message by the eye contact they give you.

Great eye contact and positive facial expressions will energize you. Look directly at those individuals, finish a thought, and move on to another person.

4. Find Friendly Faces in the Audience

There are people "loving" your Elevator Speech! They're listening to every word, and soaking up everything you're presenting.

These folks will energize you! Find one, make eye contact, and talk directly to them until you've finished a thought. Then, move on to another friendly face.

If you find a Blank Face, they probably like what they're seeing and hearing, but everyone doesn't express their likes and dislikes in the same manner. Don't worry about them, and move on, looking for that friendly face and/or one that is giving body language that they are **GETTING IT!**

You'll never make a super connection with the entire audience. Everyone brings "stuff" that is going on in their lives to the event that can have an influence on their attention to your presentation. If you find someone giving you a face of dissatisfaction, anger, or sleepiness - Move On! Not everyone will **GET IT!** That's fine.

5. Deep Breathing Exercises

Try this exercise, please:
> Count to three, take a deep breath, and sigh!
> You feel better, don't you!

We sigh when we're upset or angry. Doing so, eases that stress.

Deep Breathing is *formalized sighing*. There are several different ways of doing this, and I encourage you to explore a few.

One very simple Deep Breathing Exercise that works for me is:
- Breathe in deeply to the count of six.
- Exhale completely to the count of eight.

Practice this before attending a function where you'll have the "Speaking Opportunity" to deliver your Elevator Speech. Experiment and find a method that works for you.

6. Get a Good Night's Sleep!

When we're thoroughly rested, we work better. Our mind is sharper, and we perform better. Don't underestimate this and get plenty of sleep before attending a function where you'll have the opportunity to give your Elevator Speech.

7. Exercise

I'm a walker, and walking gets my endorphins going and mind functioning at it's best. I developed and practiced some of the best parts of my Elevator Speech when going for a power walk. (I always carry a small digital recorder with me and use it to capture things to add or fine tune in my presentations.)

Any kind of regular exercise will keep your mind sharp and body healthy.

When you look and feel well, you'll have more confidence in the presentation you'll be delivering. Your energy level will be going *up*, and your stress level will going *down*.

8. Meditation

United States Major James Nesmith was a prisoner of war in North Vietnam for seven years. Every day, for four hours, he played eighteen holes of golf.
Summer, winter, fall, and spring - every day - four hours - eighteen holes of golf.

Good weather - bad weather; it didn't matter.

He did this in his mind's eye!

When he was released from prison, and returned to the course in Southern California that he had been "playing," he cut twenty strokes off his best game! That's the power of the Mind!

Napoleon Hill is famous for saying, "Whatever the mind of man can conceive, he can achieve."

"Picture"
The audience intensely listening to your presentation.
Positive eye contact, facial expressions and body language coming from them.
Yourself at ease and enjoying delivering your talk.

Practice, in your "Mind's Eye," your Elevator Speech. Don't practice just the words, but practice all the verbal and nonverbal elements of the delivery of a great presentation. It is one of the most beneficial things you can do.

Try it in the evening before you go to sleep so it can "percolate" in your brain. You will be amazed at the results!

And, if Meditation doesn't work, try. . .

9. Medication

Sometimes the chemistry of our bodies makes it almost impossible to work on the fundamentals of a speech because the Fear of Public Speaking is so great.

There are prescription medications, called beta blockers. They reduce anxiety so a person can work on the Content and Delivery of a Presentation or Elevator Speech.

There's nothing wrong with doing this! I coached an extremely motivated doctor who couldn't move forward with her speaking until the anxiety was controlled. She sought out another doctor. That one prescribed the proper medicine and dosage, and she's doing great!

Others seek, and receive help from, hypnosis. Some find psychotherapy, from a professional, can get to the root of the fear and relieve it.

The important thing, if your fear is preventing you from moving forward, is to find something that works.

10. Cotton Mouth

Cotton mouth is no fun!

Your mouth is as dry as, well, cotton! It's not fun to have, and hard to talk with that condition. Not being able to speak intensifies anxiety.

Being nervous is one of several things that can lead to cotton mouth. Antihistamines, certain scripts, and dry air are others.

It's an uncomfortable feeling that only gets worse and adds to anxiety if it can't be relieved.

Always have room temperature water available. Water that's too hot or too cold will affect the vocal cords adversely.

Another way to get relief is to place a small lozenge between your cheek and gum. Experiment with this before the "real thing" to get the "flavor" of how it works.

Lemon or menthol flavors are best because cherry may make your mouth look like it's bleeding!

Chewing gum is not a good idea. Chewing gum looks like you're chewing gum, and that can be a distraction.

11. Practice - Practice - Practice!

Every four years the Olympics is held somewhere. Does anyone think those great athletes just "Show Up" for their big game, match, or meet?

Of course not! Many have left families and sacrificed years of their life to the hard work of preparing for those prestigious games.

How about professional singers, actors, and musicians? Do you think they just "Show Up" for their important show, play, or concert?

No-o-o!
>   Practice! - practice! - practice!
>   Rehearsal after rehearsal after rehearsal.

Even bands that have been together for over thirty years will rehearse before going on stage.

Why would someone think you could just stand up at an event and "Wing It" when delivering your Elevator Speech?

Bottom line - you can't!

You Must Practice:
- ➡ Practice your Elevator Speech into an audio recorder.
  - Is your voice loud and clear?

- Are you speaking distinctly or are some words being mumbled?
  - What is the pacing of your delivery?
- → Make a video recording of yourself.
  - Critically evaluate it.
  - Make adjustments
  - Record, again.
  - Repeat.
- → Practice in front of a mirror.
  - Look yourself in the eye as you speak.
- → Practice in your "Mind's eye."
  - Picture the audience being interested in your presentation.
  - Picture yourself being calm and collected in your thoughts and delivery.
- → Practice in front of friends and family.
  - Ask for honest feedback.
    - Saying, "Great talk!" doesn't help you improve.

You might have heard the expression, "Practice makes perfect."
  It *doesn't!*

"Perfect practice make perfect."
  That *never happens!*

I prefer the statement,
  "The road to perfection never ends!"
So. . .
- → Practice in front of a mirror.
- → Practice by speaking into a digital recorder.
- → Video yourself.
- → Practice in front of friends and family.
- → Practice with your coach. (You *have* a coach, don't you?)
  - "Professionals *have* coaches - Amateurs *don't.*"

Practice and tweak to consistently improve your content and delivery.

I cannot overemphasize how important practicing is. However, it should not seem mechanical when you deliver your elevator speech. Struggle a bit. Appear to be thinking about your next sentence.

Rehearse - Rehearse - Rehearse so much that when you deliver your Elevator Speech, the audience will think it is *Un*rehearsed!

Rehearse - Rehearse - Rehearse so much that when you deliver your Elevator Speech, the audience will think it is *Un*-rehearsed!

12. The Golden Nugget

If you get only one idea from my writing, *this* is it -
Speak!

Speak! - Speak! - Speak!

If you want to be a master baker - *Bake!*
If you want to be a competitive swimmer - *Swim!*

If you want to be a great speaker - *Speak!*

"The Learning is in the Doing!"

You can do all the intellectualizing you want about giving a great Elevator Speech.
- Read books and articles.
- Watch videos.
- Listen to audio recordings.
- Observe other speakers.
- Practice in your mind's eye.

The real Learning is in the Doing!

There's no easy way, and nothing beats the real thing.

Deliver Your Elevator Speech
- In front of friends and family.
- To Chambers of Commerce.
- To Lion Clubs, Rotaries, Optimists, and other organizations where they regularly have outside speakers.

Do it as often as you can!

What's the worse that could happen?
➡The baker's cake falls.
➡The swimmer comes in last.
➡The speaker bombs.
  • Big Deal!
  • Who Cares!
  • It's a drop in the ocean of your life. It's *nothing!*

Each time you do it you'll learn something and improve. When results start coming in, you'll see your hard work paying off. You'll also feel better about yourself for having accomplished something most struggle with.

Chapter 9 - Failure Gets a Bad Rap

Have you ever Failed?

Of course!

Now think of a *specific* time you Failed.

Question:
Did you learn more from that Failure, or from something that went exactly the way you wanted it to the first time you tried it?

For myself, if I get something correct the first time - it's usually dumb luck! If that does happen, you're probably like me and don't make a Mental Template that says, "If this ever occurs, I'll do that." Correct?

In instances like that, we really don't learn anything, we just *luck out.*

We learn *far more* from our failures than from our successes. Failing is really a *good* thing.

Why then, are we so afraid of Failing?

Maybe it's the word - **Failure.** We take it *personally.*
Even some of **Definitions of Failure** are:

1. Lack of success.
2. An unsuccessful person.

That's crazy and nonproductive!

Perhaps we need to forget the word, **Failure**, and substitute the word, **Experiment**. We don't expect experiments to always give the results we are seeking.

Thomas Edison, so the story goes, did over 10,000 experiments before inventing the incandescent light bulb.

A newspaper reporter asked Thomas Edison, "How does it feel to have failed 10,000 times in your search for the electric light bulb?"

The genius inventor replied: "I have not failed. I've just found 10,000 ways that won't work."

That's the mindset to have, *isn't it?*

One Formula for Success is:
- Fail *Early.*
- Fail *Often.*
- Fail *Quickly.*
- Sometimes, *Fail BIG!*

Go BIG, or Go Home!

Failure gets a Bad Rap. We should be *embracing* it.

I'm fond of basketball's great Michael Jordan's take on Failure. He said,

- "I missed more than 9,000 shots in my career.
- I've lost almost 300 games.
- Twenty-six times I've been trusted to take the game winning shot - and missed.
- I've failed over and over and over again in my life.
- That is why I *succeed.*"

The only *real* failure is *not* failing. Think about it!

When? - Why? - Where?

I remember when one of my grandson's, Carson, not quite one year old at the time, was visiting our home. He wasn't walking yet, but he was *trying!*

If you've ever observed a baby learning to walk you know what a great lesson in persistence it is. It reminds me of that great quote from the Apollo 13 Movie, "Failure is not an option!"

Carson would pull himself up using a coffee table we have in our living room. I watched him get his balance, then surf a step or two, to the right. You've seen this, haven't you? He kept his hands on the table, and moved his legs gingerly, side by side. He'd let go with one hand, giving us a big, proud smile. Next, he'd let go the other hand. He'd stand on his own for a second or two, then - boom! He'd fall down.

He'd sit on the floor for a moment or two, didn't cry, then pull himself up, again. I'd watch a big smile come over his face as he got his balance, moved a step or two sideways, let go with one hand, then the other and - fall down!

Smiling, as he sat on the floor, he would. . .

Well, you can see where I'm going with this, can't you?

When - Why - and *Where,* as we're growing up, do we decide if we fall down, we won't *immediately* pull ourselves up - *and try, again?*

I *Guarantee*

The *Worst* Speech You'll *Ever* Give, Will be Far Better than the One you *Never* Give!"

That's worth repeating!

The *worst* Elevator Speech you'll *ever* give, will be far better than the one you *never* give!

Chapter 10 - Conclusion

Review

Let's review the Goal of an Elevator Speech.

It is *not* a sales presentation.

The Goal, as in all communication, is for the recipients, be it an individual or a large group, to **GET IT!** They should have a *clear* understanding of *who* you are and *what* you do.

Ideally, we would like them to want more information on our offerings, for themselves, or someone they believe can use our products and services. Having them asking for a future conversation is usually a good thing!

Building your Elevator Speech, Floor-by-floor, gives the flexibility to modify it for different audiences and time considerations.

In a One-on-one situation, instead of using it to *Qualify* prospects, use it to *Dis*qualify, or eliminate persons you're speaking with and people they know. Then, as time permits, move on to another person on your Target List.

As important as the content of the Floors of your Elevator Speech is, the Delivery is *more* important. Your content could be excellent, but if it's not delivered in a manner that educates and explains *who* you are and *what* you do, they won't **GET IT!**

As previously stated, your Delivery has two parts; Verbal and NonVerbal. Since "we believe what we see," NonVerbal trumps Verbal. Review this section of the book several times.

Close

I'm going to close with a **Challenge** and a **Prediction**.

Here's my Challenge:
Craft an Elevator Speech using this template and your Elevator Speech Worksheet. Put it in your world using your words.

Practice it - Tweak it
Practice it - Tweak it
Practice - Practice - Practice.
Attend an event where the host says, "Before we get started, let's go around the room and introduce ourselves. Tell us who you are and what you do. Give us your Elevator Speech."

Do *that*, and **my Prediction is *this*:**
You won't panic. You won't wish you were elsewhere.

When you stand to speak, delivering your Elevator Speech *will* be: absolutely, positively, there's no doubt in my mind, no ifs, ands, or buts, about it - that mini-presentation will be - *NO SWEAT!*

The Elevator Speech Template

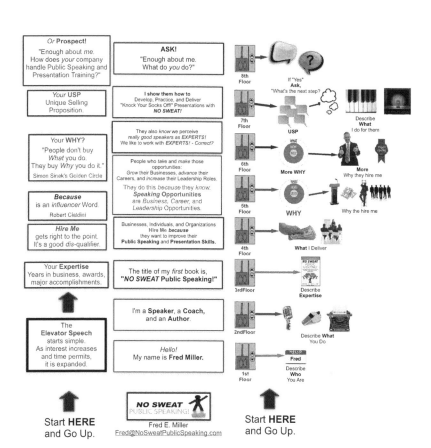

Start **HERE**
and Go Up.

NO SWEAT
PUBLIC SPEAKING!
Fred E. Miller
Fred@NoSweatPublicSpeaking.com

Start **HERE**
and Go Up.

YOUR Elevator Speech Worksheet

Build It One Floor at a Time - **Start at the _Bottom_ and Work Your Way _Up!_**

Fred Miller -
Fred@NoSweatPublicSpeaking.com

8th Floor **Ask!**

Either ask what _they_ do, or Ask by bringing the subject back to you

(This floor can sometimes be skipped in the "Group Audience" Elevator Speech.)

7th Floor **What You Do for Them!**

Your **USP**, Unique Selling Proposition.

6th Floor More Information on **_Why_ they hire me.**
(This floor can sometimes be skipped.)

5th Floor _Your_ **WHY.**

People don't buy _what_ you do. They buy **_WHY_ you do it."**

4th Floor **What** *you* Deliver. **Why** they hire *you*.

3rd Floor What is your **Expertise?**

2nd Floor Describe **What** you do.

1st. Floor **Who** you are. (Your Name.)

One More Thing. . .

Steve Jobs, my presentation hero, would often *semi-close* Keynote Presentations with this statement. He would then rock the audience with the introduction of, yet another, great apple product or service.

He was the consummate presenter. I've learned a great deal by watching his videos and reading books and articles about his presentation skills.

It is with the deepest respect and humility that I write, **One More Thing. . .**

That **One More Thing** is that I'd like to hear from *you!*

- Send me *your* Elevator Speech!
- Visit my blog and, if you're inclined, post a comment. Agree or disagree, I eagerly await reading your thoughts.

Feel free to contact me with your questions, suggestions, speaking accomplishments, and, yes, if you have them, **Speaking Opportunities!**

Fred E. Miller
Fred@NoSweatPublicSpeaking.com
www.NoSweatPublicSpeaking.com

FREE Gifts!

I have **Two FREE Gifts** for you!

1. The **Elevator Speech Template,** as a PDF, that goes hand-in-glove with this book.
2. An **Elevator Speech Worksheet,** as a PDF, that has space on each "Floor" to fill in *your* information.

Working with these will help you develop a *great* Elevator Speech with - *NO SWEAT!*

Go here to receive them **FREE**

http://www.NoSweatPublicSpeaking.com/
go/FreeEelevatorSpeechTemplate

Was this book helpful? If so, check out the following *NO SWEAT!* books.

"*NO SWEAT* Public Speaking!"

"The Fear of Public Speaking! Why? & Nuggets to Lessen It with - *NO SWEAT!*"

Both can be found here:
https://www.amazon.com/author/fredemiller

NO SWEAT ELEVATOR SPEECH
is also available as a downloadable audio book from Audible.com, Amazon, and iTunes.

Click <u>Here</u> to Order.

57216585R00063

Made in the USA
Columbia, SC
06 May 2019